GLIMPSES

A FULL EVENING OF THEATRE: SCENES, DRAMATIC MONOLOGUES & SHORT PLAYLETS

by some very talented young playwrights

THE DRAMATIC PUBLISHING COMPANY

This volume contains the work of young American playwrights. It was in no way edited, censored or re-worked by the adults directing the project. Those who experienced the artistic fulfillment generated by the project hope other young people might enjoy mounting these pieces in productions of their own. Further, it is hoped these new productions will include new work submitted by future producing organizations.

The Original Project: Walden Theatre, Louisville, Kentucky. Walden Theatre Playwright-in-Residence, Vaughn McBride, conducted tutorial sessions once weekly, at which only the writers were present. During these sessions, lasting approximately two hours, monologue as well as dialogue form was discussed. Topics running the gamut from news stories to color tones were assigned. Writing time was then allowed, and open discussion was invited on the resulting work.

Once weekly, following these tutorials, Nancy Niles Sexton, Producing Director of Walden Theatre, conducted workshop sessions where the writers were joined by young actors, directors and stage managers. Again, the pieces were read, discussed and open criticism encouraged. The pieces selected by this group were then given workshop staging, often resulting in necessary re-writing, additions and new focus demanded by theatricality. Again the work progressed through tutorial sessions and back to workshop staging.

In the fifth month, production teams were selected primarily by the choices of the group: a young director asking a writer if he might work with the piece in question or an actor requesting an opportunity to work on a piece that subjectively touched a chord within. Then, in the sixth month, the pieces were performed on a double bill playing in repertory on weekends only. A third bill was performed in March as part of the Humana Festival of New American Plays at Actors Theatre of Louisville during "critics' weekend." The following script is arranged to reflect the original ordering for Bill One and Bill Two. Those pieces selected for Bill Three are noted at the individual introductory page preceding the piece, with the number they held in the order of the bill. Also included in the script are several pieces not performed in the original production. Substitutions or additions for future production are encouraged out of this new material. It is also hoped that new productions would include work newly written by performing groups.

The Performing Space: The original performing space was a large hall with a three-sided thrust stage fashioned out of small raised platforms along the back of a 30' by 20' rug. The script is extremely adaptable to any space, be it an open hall, a large proscenium stage or classroom. No stage setting is required.

Required Set Pieces: Stools and folding chairs were used in the original production, as well as one simple wooden table strong enough to be sat upon. These set pieces were moved and struck by the actors as the work progressed. The needs for each individual piece are noted on the page preceding each piece.

Costumes and Properties: Most of the material was performed without any special costume but rather in clothes from the actor's own wardrobe that reflected the fashion modes of contemporary youth that the company felt suitable to each piece as it was performed. Special costume needs are noted on the page preceding each piece, if necessary to the material. Several pieces demanded hand properties and they also are noted. In both costume and props, simple choices should be made.

Lighting: The original production was done with three major lighting special areas: UR, C and DLC. These areas are noted in the script as areas 1, 2 and 3. The general stage lighting was done with nine over-lapping areas.

Music: Each of the pieces was performed with lead-in music selected from the vast canon of classical and contemporary scores. It was a company choice and is not included by name in the script. Rather, each future performing company is encouraged to select their own score that they feel best reflects the mood of their work. Therefore, each cue is marked, but no specific musical piece is selected.

NOTICE

GLIMPSES appears here in its original form, uncensored and unedited.

There are thirty-two "glimpses" and you may use all of them for your production or make choices among them. (The choices made by The Walden Theatre for three separate productions are listed on the following page.)

A few of the pieces contain expletives. If you feel that any of them are not appropriate for your production but you still want to include that particular "glimpse," you have the playwright's permission to delete any unacceptable word or phrase.

It is important to note, however, that all the included pieces were openly discussed in both tutorials and workshop sessions from all points of view. It was clearly felt, in all cases, that the work reflects an unwaivering address to truth and realism as the young company saw it to be.

GLIMPSES, in all its parts, mirrors its times.

CONTENTS

The short pieces in this playbook have been presented by Walden Theatre in the following groupings:

(Listed in order of appearance on each bill.)

Your group may wish to present one of the above bills or create a new bill by choosing a different grouping or a different order, or by mixing these pieces with "glimpses" of your own.

BILL ONE

Pre-set: Choice of Director/Designer.

THE ADOLESCENT FUGUE
By Ruth Jacobson

Bill One:	No. 1
Bill Two:	--
Bill Three:	No. 3
Lighting:	Full Stage
Music:	Classical Fugue
Costume:	See script
Props:	See script
Setting:	See script

Humorous
Three Females/Two Males

CAST

Becky Jo Turner	A preppy high school junior. Very full of her own self-importance. Pamela Westmore's best friend.
Jim James	Twelve years old and into mischief.
Chordrice James	Jim's older sister. Not too popular, but in love with Les Douglas.
Les Douglas	Most popular boy at school. In love with Pamela Westmore.
Cloris	A thin girl who thinks she's fat. She would like Chordrice James to be her friend.

SETTING

UR is a small stool for Jim James. His area is littered with old Coke cans, candy wrappers, potato chip bags. Also there are various magazines: *Playboy, Field & Stream, Sports Illustrated.* DR is a chair and stool with a phone on it. Also on the stool beside the phone is a huge Hershey chocolate bar. UC is a large chair for Les. All about him is a litter of clothes — dirty socks, tennis shoes, shirts, etc. He is eating an apple and sits very casually without a shirt, socks or shoes. DL is a table with a chair. On the table are half-eaten McDonald's things — Big Mac, fries, Coke, etc. UL is Cloris' area to exercise in.

At the opening, JIM JAMES is UR, CHORDRICE moves DR, LES is at C, CLORIS is UL, BECKY JO is DC.

BECKY. Hi. My name is Becky Jo Turner, and I'm a student at Ferndale High. I've been class president two years in a row now, and I'm on the honor roll. Well, I guess that's about it.

CHORDRICE. If I, Chordrice James, had to say what the worst thing on earth was, it would have to be brothers. My older one always thinks he knows everything and my younger one gets away with murder and pins it on me. Little brat.

JIM. Hi. My name is, uh, Jim. I'm twelve. Heh, heh . . . I'm sorry I'm so dead but whooo . . . last night me and some friends got so *drunk* . . . got us some beer and split it up . . . I don't remember *anything* . . . hee! hee!

CLORIS. God, I hate being fat. I mean, fat is so ugly, y'know? People hate fat, they laugh at fat, fat makes them sick. It makes *me* sick. It's like a big, quivering tumor all over your body. That's what I really hate about fat . . . the way you jiggle. I can't run in public without the whole town snickering, "Did you see Cloris run, isn't it a riot?" I can't wear anything tighter than a burlap sack without drawing glances and giggles. I've never been popular. I've had maybe two true friends.

JIM. Me and my best friend Denny, we always get loaded on weekends.

BECKY. I know I look really bad. You don't have to tell me. I didn't wash my hair today and my make-up is just a *mess*. I hate these clothes, too . . . they're almost two years old. My mother is such a tightwad . . .

LES. I guess you could say I'm popular. I always have a girl friend. I always know any girl would die to go out with me. I mean, let's face it — I am good-looking. But popularity can be a pain in the ass.

JIM. It's fun! We sneak some beer out of his parents' refrigerator and get so drunk! Last night we were all yellin' and stuff . . . it was really fun. We had some AC/DC and Van Halen cassettes and played 'em and it was just a blast! We were gonna call up some girls in our class but we didn't really feel like it.

CHORDRICE. I hate my brothers *so* much! They always make

10

fun of my zits. I do have acne, but do they have to remind me? I always call 'em zits because they don't deserve a better name. Why did God make zits? I mean, he could have just never invented them and everyone would do just fine. I tell myself not to eat chocolate but I do anyway — I love chocolate! That's like with my braces . . . I can't chew gum! I just said, up yours! Do you know how boring life would be without chocolate or gum? I'd rather not think about it.

CLORIS. God, look at me!

BECKY. I tell my mother everyone has new clothes . . .

CLORIS. I'm an object of ridicule, a freak!

BECKY. . . . or at least only a year old . . .

CLORIS. People look at me and say, how could any human being be so big and do this to herself?

BECKY. . . . but *no one* wears clothes that old . . . except maybe my grandmother.

LES. Take my girl friend, for instance — Pamela. She's really great-looking and wears nice clothes and has this mole on her cheek that really turns me on. But she doesn't have anything between her ears! She's a vacuum-head, y'know?

CHORDRICE. I know who I *would* rather think of . . . Les Douglas! He is the biggest fox in my whole school! He has the greatest body, and his legs are already hairy and everything! God! I would give my life to have a date with Les Douglas.

CLORIS. Well, I'll tell you. You aren't that pretty to begin with, you get your feelings hurt, you start to eat. You eat because it tastes good, you eat because the food comforts you. You eat and eat, saying so-and-so is fatter, and she gets dates.

BECKY. I saw this cute little purse at Pembley's, but it was sixty dollars. I begged my mother to take me back, but would she? No! She had to go get *her* clothes first! She always gets to buy all these clothes and I hardly get any! Sure, I could wear hers, but who wants to wear your *mother's* clothes? If anyone said, "I like your sweater, where'd you get it?" I would just *die*!

11

JIM. I got a girl friend, by the way. She's real tall, taller than me, and boy! Does she have big ones! Hee! Hee! Her name is Cindi, with an "i" at the end. She writes me notes in class and she always makes her "i's" with big hollow dots. I think it's kinda cute.

CHORDRICE. Of course, he doesn't know me, but there's always hope, right? Right now he's going with this sleaze-ball, Pamela Westmore.

BECKY. And my dad isn't any better. I asked him for a raise in my allowance, and would he do it? Of *course* not! He said five dollars is enough. A mouse couldn't live on five dollars! God! My parents! I don't know where they came from . . . a dinosaur egg, probably!

CLORIS. Then you get fatter than all the so-and-so's and you realize it, all of a sudden. Looking in the mirror makes you sick. You dread getting dressed up, shopping, and summer. You cry lots of lonely, boring Saturday nights when you're all alone.

JIM. Denny 'n' me are gonna try out for football together. I'm kinda little, but I can beat up any guy I want. I can. I beat up this one kid, gave him a black eye 'n' a bloody nose, and he was bawlin' . . . hee! hee! hee!

LES. Not that she's any different. All the girls I know are real spacey. The ones who have anything sensible to say are dogs. Some of them are ugly *and* stupid. There's this one girl who just stares at me all day long in class. She has all these pimples and braces − and this really weird name − Clorice or some-thing. She always watches my butt until I feel like a hunk of meat or something.

CLORIS. You never go on dates. I haven't, not once. Once I got leered at by a drunk. I am seventeen and I have not been kissed, or held, or hugged by any member of the opposite sex except my father! I just want to scream sometimes, I just want to be loved so badly!

CHORDRICE. Ooh, she's such a slime bag! She wears the dumbest clothes and her hair is in one of those curly perms . . .

12

oh, it looks *okay*, I guess, but her nose is kind of crooked and she has this *mole* on the side of her cheek that I think is positively disgusting. I mean, it doesn't have hairs growing out of it or anything, but still . . . I don't think Les likes her that much anyway. But he'll never go for me . . .

BECKY. We have to do an English paper on Withering Heights by tomorrow. I hope I'll do okay on it . . . Ms. Grilstone *usually* gives me "A" 's but Withering Heights is so hard to read! I mean, not that I *couldn't* but I did skip some parts. It was so *bo-ring*.

JIM. When I grow up I'm gonna be a forest ranger. I like animals an' birds an' trees an' stuff. They're cute.

BECKY. Pamela Westmore is my best friend. Her middle name is Jo, too, isn't that weird? Her hair is always *so cute*! She got a perm the other day and it looks so good! She's really pretty. She went to Amazon Modeling Agency and that is expensive. My dumb parents won't let me go! She said she really looked gross until she went there. I wish my parents weren't so stupid! I want to be a model and everything but they still won't let me go! *God*!

CLORIS. I suppose you think I feel sorry for myself. You're right. I do. But look at me, really hard — Cloris the Freak, Cloris the Fat Lady — and then ask yourself — do you blame me?

JIM. Y'know what? Heh, heh. My name ain't really Jim. It's Walter. Walter James, see? I hate my parents! Why'd they hafta gimme some dumb name like Walter? It's embarrassing! In school, substitutes always read it out loud an' everyone laughs. That's why I gave that kid a black eye . . . he was laughing at my name. Well, it wasn't really a black eye . . . it was just red for a little while . . . But I gave him a bloody nose all right! Heh! Heh!

LES. You should see some of the losers that really think I'd go out with them. It's almost a joke! Tall, short, fat, scrawny, stupid, ugly, from dishwater blonde to mousey brunette! Every variety of pimple known to man. And they all wear

13

padded bras and brush up against you in the hall . . . I don't know. All I have to say about it is this — thank God there's some intelligent *men* to talk to. Girls can drive anyone up a wall.

(Actors repeat their last line to create a vocal fugue. Music repeats.)

LIGHTS ALL FADE

THE BOOKWORM
By Ruth Jacobson

Bill One: No. 2

Bill Two: --

Bill Three: --

Lighting: Area 2

Music: Fade out on Fugue

Costume: No special

Props: No special

Setting: See script

Humorous
Male or Female

(An ACTOR enters, crosses to C stage, and speaks.)

ACTOR. There is only one vocation where every member of it fits a stereotype. That is the vocation of librarian.

Librarians are women. They are asexual or frigid. They *do* wear their hair in buns. They *don't* have lips.

I believe on an application for a librarian's position it asks if you can fulfill these requirements. It must. They also must decide on uniforms. Maybe they shop together. They all wear sensible shoes and prim little jumpers and pantsuits, and they all stare you down if you drop a book or something.

They must get all librarians from hospital wards. They look so pinched and dead. But most of all, they have no personality. Their life is books and rules and dust. No wonder they all act the same. What kind of person would want a job like that?

THE ORANGE TABLECLOTH
By Traci Nall

Bill One:	No. 3
Bill Two:	--
Bill Three:	--
Lighting:	Crossfade from special No. 2 to area DL
Music:	Contemporary
Costume:	No special
Props:	See script
Setting:	See script

Serious
Female

(Small, lighted space reveals a table and one chair. ACTRESS enters light, touches top of table gently as in memory. She speaks to audience.)

ACTRESS. When I was in the sixth grade, the thing that I remember most was the tablecloth on the table in the lunchroom. It was a dirty, plastic, orange.

At that time, it seemed, the girls hung around with the girls and the guys stayed mostly around the other guys. Oh, I don't know why. Maybe we were just shy or something. During lunch the boys would all sit at one end of the table and the girls at the other. Unless a chair was missing or someone was just taking up a lot of space, there would always be an extra chair and an extra space for a person between the girls' and the boys' side. If you were the poor person who had to sit in the middle, right next to that empty space, you could never hear what all the other girls were laughing about or just talking about. Unfortunately, I was the one who sat next to the empty chair and empty space. I think it was because I could never get my locker open and put my books in fast enough to get to the lunchroom before all the good seats were taken, so I would sit down, open my lunch bag and try to talk to the person sitting next to me. But she would usually be too busy trying to listen to the one near the head of the table. So there I would be, slowly chewing my peanut butter and jelly sandwich, staring down at the dirty, orange plastic tablecloth.

LIGHTS SLOWLY DIM

FLUFFY
By Ruth Jacobson

Bill One: No. 4

Bill Two: --

Bill Three: --

Lighting: Special No. 1

Music: Contemporary Romantic 1950's

Costume: No special

Props: See items in script

Setting: Small stool

Humorous
Female

(Fluffy's Owner has just finished writing a letter to Ann Landers. She sighs, then reads aloud as she signs:)

FLUFFY'S OWNER. "Heartsick in Virginia." (She picks up her letter carefully and reads what she has written.) "Dear Ann: I have been crying since two o'clock this afternoon. Maybe this letter will make some people think twice before they go out of their way to hit a poor, defenseless creature, just for the fun of it. (Slight pause.) We live on a busy street. My pet cat Fluffy has crossed this street dozens of times. Nothing ever happened to her until this morning. I saw a driver in a small car deliberately go out of his way to hit Fluffy. If he had gone in a straight line, Fluffy would be alive today. But, no, that horrible murderer made a sharp turn and killed my pet. I know you can't do anything about those sicko creeps out there, but I had to write this letter in memory of one of the dearest joy-givers in the world. — Heartsick in Virginia."

When I found out what happened . . . I just . . . collapsed. She had always been my dearest friend, my confidante, and then she was . . . gone! My darling little kitty, my precious, my Fluffy! She was such a poor, defenseless creature! What did she ever do to harm anybody? If anyone should ever have wanted to kill my little Fluffy, it would have been a mouse or a bird. Fluffy always caught lots of them. I couldn't understand it, but I could *maybe* forgive them if they hurt her. But someone who'd never seen her, never petted Fluffy or even knew she was alive, how could they run her over in the street like she was a dog or something?

I never was cross with her — she was such a sweet kitty. If someone came to the house, she was *always* a little, well, *shy* but she never seriously wounded *anyone*! Except, of course, the one time my ex-fiance came over for the first time . . .

20

When I first got Fluffy, she was so adorble! She'd look up into your face with those deep blue eyes of hers and that fluffy white fur — that was why I named her Fluffy, she was such a little ball of fluff — and then she'd nip at your finger wth her pointy little teeth — but she was only playing! When she got older she would sleep in bed with me. She was such a cutie, she always hissed if you got on to her half of the bed! It got to where I would fix meals for my Fluffy so she would eat what I ate. I even got a bunch of little cat clothes — a little coat, a morning dress, a bathrobe, a whole bunch of stuff, even a little Santa suit for Christmas. She never wore them, but sometimes I could convince her to put on the coat. It looked so adorable with her coloring, it was the exact color of her eyes.

But now Fluffy is gone — killed by some heartless cad! Perhaps it's better that she died a quick death, though. I doubt she could have lived through the trauma. She had such a delicate constitution.

Well, I've been looking into pet funerals. I want to give Fluffy the best. I called the morgue to see if they could keep her but they hung up so now she's in my refrigerator. The poor darling is smelling up the place rather badly. But I want to give my Fluffy the best. God knows she deserves it.

NOT JUST SINGIN'
By Michael Weiss

Bill One:	No. 5
Bill Two:	--
Bill Three:	No. 9
Lighting:	DL area
Music:	Reprise from last piece
Costume:	No special.
Props:	Broom and bucket.
Setting:	Table/chair.

Serious
Female

(Light comes up to reveal an empty stage. A young black
ACTRESS enters with pail and broom. She begins to speak.)

ACTRESS. I'm tired. Cleaning is my job. It's what I've done my
whole life. Offices. Homes. I've never made any money to
speak of, but I'm comfortable. I've got my church and my
friends from church. Greater Salem Baptist Church. It's
my whole life. I'm an usher there. Every Sunday I put on
my uniform and I lead the choir down the aisle to the pulpit.
Hurt my ankle last year and had to quit for a while, but I'm
back now.

I do more than just usher though. I sing. The first time I
sang in church I was four years old. Everybody at church
said I should take up singin' as a professional. I've always
known I could sing – good! – but I'd say that gettin' up in
front of crowds makes me nervous, and it does.

People still ask me to sing in Sunday services, and I do a
couple times every year. When I'm walkin' up to the pulpit,
I always feel like my shoes are makin' too much noise, hittin'
that wood floor – it's so quiet, everybody waitin' for me to
sing. Sometime I'll tell them how nervous I am. My heart's
beatin' a thousand times a minute. Then I just start up singin'
whenever I'm ready. (She sings an inspirational song:)
   "Please be patient with me;
   God is not through with me yet . . ."

I'm the voice of the Lord. When I sing, I don't pay attention
to anything else, just feel. A feeling I get only when I sing.
Chills go up my back, my cheeks tighten up, and I don't feel
anything around me. I become removed. Replaced by the
Lord Jesus Christ. Everybody out there knows it, too. They
cry 'cause they know Jesus Christ's inside my body when I
sing. They cry happy tears – the men, too. They feel what I
feel. So much joy and understandin' comin' out of those

23

notes, me and everybody listenin' cry them salty tears. Them tears come out of our bodies along with our sinful ways. Badness leaving our souls. . . . I don't take credit. Jesus gets it. I just start singin' and He takes over. I'm not sorry for not going after singin' as a callin'. Singin' in church is enough for me.

I was married at fifteen. I met him in Athens. Athens, Alabama. Knew him before I . . . well, before I became a woman. Just a little girl and already in love. I was so shy . . . everybody, everybody knew Jackson. And they all said the same thing. "He's the goodest man in the world, till he gets to drinkin'." He did a lot of that. When he got to drinkin' he was mean as a bull. Alcohol made the devil come out of my husband's soul.

About five months after we were married . . . Jackson shot his friend, Joe Bill Wilson. A lousy eight dollars Joe Bill owed him from some card game. Blew a hole in his chest. He brought me with him to go collect his money . . . I didn't know nothin', didn't have the sense not to get in that ol' truck. Jackson could hardly keep the thing on the dirt road to town. We run up with Joe Bill about five miles outside of town. He was in his pickup headin' the other way. Jackson blocked the road with the car so Joe Bill had to stop. I wasn't gonna leave the seat of that ol' truck of Jackson's for nothing'. There was no tellin' what Jackson would do when he got to drinkin'.

Joe Bill said he didn't have the eight dollars and he wasn't gonna pay up no way. So . . . Jackson cocked that gun and blew a hole in Joe Bill's chest. I got out to tend the bleedin', but it was too late . . . my husband said, "Girl, get back in this car." I said "no." He tried to force me in, but somehow I broke loose of his big hand that was tight around my arm. I broke loose and I ran. Jackson got out of the car and flew off

24

after me. Running, running, running after me. He got hold of my arm again and threw me down, hard. Layin' in a field with a bunch of dead grass and nobody around to help me. I yelled anyway. "Help!" I yelled. "Help. Help me! Help!" I knew he was gonna hurt me. I could see it in his eyes. Crazy, crazy he was while he pulled his whittlin' knife out of the leather sheath that he always wore on his belt. That knife that I saw every day and sometimes used it to cut up vegetables was gonna stick in me. I laid there. I laid there while he raised that knife high above his head. Down, down, down it came. That knife catchin' the light of the hot sun and findin' a place in my body, my stomach. It's bleedin', bleedin' bad. Lord! Lord! You'll help me, won't you? Help me, Lord. Protect me from the devil. The devil, Lord.

. . . I'm alone now, prob'ly better off for it. The cut's been healed for a long time. Just a scar now. A scar that's so's I remember that day. That day when I met the devil. The devil inside my husband that I never wanta see again.

In the scripture, it says how Jesus was nailed up to that cross at his hands and feet. Well, I thought a lot about that. Jesus got a hole poked in his body like I did. Well, not the same way and all, but we both felt the pain. He died from it, but I didn't. I lived on to see the scar in the place where a knife laid in my body. Somehow it all helps me. When I get up and sing for the church, I start to singin' and I think about that scar, and I feel Jesus. Oh, God, God, there you are. I hear you, God, I hear you. (She sings inspirational song again.)
"Please be patient with me;
God is not through with me yet . . . "

LIGHTS DIM TO OUT

YELLOW SNOWBALLS
By Michael Weiss

Bill One:	No. 6
Bill Two:	--
Bill Three:	--
Lighting:	Special No. 1
Music:	Circus Music
Costume:	An apron with bib
Props:	No special
Setting:	See script

Serious
Female

(Fair music plays as a GIRL moves into small lighted space. Music fades as she speaks.)

GIRL. I sell snowballs at the county fair. It comes in town every year and I sell snowballs every year. It's snow, spelled "s-n-o." They leave out the "w" . . . it's more catchy that way. Yep, there's a big sign above the booth that's got "Snoballs" written on it. The letters are painted on so it looks like there's ice hangin' off 'em.

"Get your cold snowballs, cool and delicious cherry, grape and orange." That's what I yell out to the crowd walkin' by if business has gotten slow for awhile. Ha! Ha! Then some child will come up to me and hand me a bunch of pennies for a cone with all three flavors on it. Even if they're a few pennies short, I'll give them their cones.

Cones. Oh, we just call 'em cones for short. Cones are more fun than anything else. People walk away from the booth laughin', carryin' on and havin' a good time. Or sometimes just smilin', but still havin' a good time and there I am, standin' on the other side of that wood board next to my cone machine. It's whirlin' away makin' little pieces of crushed ice and I get all caught up in the whole fair until my eyes start to water, my face starts to tingle, and all I can think about are good things. Happy, happy I get as the clean white ice piles up in little mountains inside the cone machine.

"Get your snowballs, cool and delicious cherry, grape and orange." If they ask me for extra syrup flavoring, I always give it to 'em. When I buy cones from other people, they're always so weak. They don't put enough cherry, grape and orange flavoring in.

When the fair is in town, it's my happiest time of year. Everybody is happy at the fair. It's like being closed up in a world

27

far away from earth. Nobody will yell at you or hurt you like when I'm away from the county fair.

I used to wish the fair lasted all year . . . just one big happy time. Yeah, I used to wish I could stay at the fair my whole life and never have to leave . . . I still do.

"Snowballs . . . get your snowballs here . . . "

LIGHTS FADE AND MUSIC COVERS

THE LAST TRAIN TO CHARLOTTESVILLE
By Robert Sexton III

Bill One:	No. 7
Bill Two:	--
Bill Three:	--
Lighting:	From special No. 2 to full stage and back to special No. 2 at close
Music:	Folk
Costume:	Simple, as the character needs
Props:	Briefcase, newspaper, signs, cane
Setting:	See script

Serious
Three Male Actors

CAST

TICKET AGENT
OLD MAN
BUSINESS MAN

(Curtain pre-set open. Lights come up on scene. Action takes place in a large train station in an industrial city in the northeast. We see a ticket window, a waiting bench, and a gate. There is a large sign saying, "To Trains." The TICKET AGENT enters and crosses stage slowly to DL and enters booth. Lighting: Special No. 2.)

TICKET AGENT. Look about you. You see before you our Municipal Union Station. It was the city's pride when it was new. Now look at it. Its beauty remains but its soul has left it. It stands here forlornly; an old lady about to receive her last caller.

(Lights slowly come up on a bench where an OLD MAN is sitting. Seated next to him is a BUSINESS MAN, reading a newspaper.)

TICKET AGENT. Well, at least there are some passengers here today. (During this dialogue, the TICKET AGENT has moved outside his booth. After he is finished speaking, he moves back inside the booth. There is absolute silence for several seconds.)
OLD MAN. Where are you going?
BUSINESS MAN. Pardon me?
OLD MAN. Where are you going?
BUSINESS MAN. New York. (Silence.)
OLD MAN. Well, aren't you going to ask me where I'm going?
BUSINESS MAN. Uh . . . well, where are you going?

OLD MAN. Charlottesville.

BUSINESS MAN. That's not too far from here, is it?

OLD MAN. Not really. Get in 'bout nine tomorrow morning. When do you get into New York?

BUSINESS MAN. Seven at night. Penn Station.

OLD MAN. I saw Penn Station once when I was about your age. I've never seen anything like it, before or since. Isn't the same any more.

BUSINESS MAN. How come?

OLD MAN. Pardon me?

BUSINESS MAN. How come it isn't the same?

OLD MAN. They tore it down and built a new one. Smaller. (Silence.) I'm going to Charlottesville to visit my sister. I may not be coming back. We've been in the habit of visiting each other twice a year. You see, my wife's passed on and her husband's passed on and when we're together we can remember the old times and forget we're just two old people.

BUSINESS MAN. Um. . . . Been on this train before?

OLD MAN. Twice a year for the last thirty years.

BUSINESS MAN. Is it a good train?

OLD MAN. It was when I first started riding it. It's gone down some since. Kinda like me, I guess.

BUSINESS MAN. I haven't been on a train since I was a little kid. I wouldn't be on one now if my doctor hadn't told me to slow down. I figured by spending four days on this trip instead of one, I could get some rest.

OLD MAN. Well, if you ask me, I think everyone should slow down. I get tired just watching everyone running around.

BUSINESS MAN. Why do you ride the train?

OLD MAN. When I first started going to Charlottesville it was the only way to go. And anyway, I always loved them . . . the trains, I mean. I've depended on this train for thirty years. I just can't quit.

BUSINESS MAN. I can see your point. (The two men fall into silence. It is interrupted by the sound of the train's arrival.)

31

TICKET AGENT. Train's in, gentlemen.

(The OLD MAN and the BUSINESS MAN shake hands and go separately to the train, through the gate. The TICKET AGENT locks it and puts a large sign in the ticket window. It reads, "All Further Passenger Service Has Been Discontinued. By Order of the General Management. P.C.R.R." He turns the light off in the ticket booth and exits R.)

LITTLE PEOPLE
By Daniel Jenkins

Bill One:	No. 8
Bill Two:	--
Bill Three:	No. 10
Lighting:	No. 1
Music:	Top borrowed from preceding piece. Bottom is contemporary.
Costume:	No special
Props:	Baseball cards
Setting:	See script

**Serious
Male**

(As lights come up, we see DAVID NORRIS leaning back on his couch, sitting on the floor in his apartment. There are several organized piles of baseball cards in front of him, a scattered pile at his side, along with a shoebox full nearby. He is drinking a glass of milk and sorting the cards by teams.)

DAVID (silently sorting for a few beats, randomly looking at the back of one). Right. How could he do that? Carl Yastrz . . . Carl Ystrem . . . this guy has had almost two hundred hits every year since nineteen sixty-two! Wow. That would be . . . a lot. Whoa! I wonder what "AB's" are. He sure has a lot of those. Huh . . . they all do. (Sorting.) Tigers . . . Tigers. "Pee Wee" Reese. Ha — "Pee Wee" Weese. Dodgers . . . Mom gave me his baseball cards. For some reason. (Still sorting.) I saw a mother on the bus today. She was holding two little kids — one in each arm — and a bag of groceries in her lap. When she got off, she had to squeeze her two cute cubs together to hold the groceries up. The kids decided it was time to eat, so they started munching on the cookies. She tried to nudge their hands away with her chin, but finally gave up — and they stumbled off leaving a trail of Oreo crumbs. White Sox . . . Phillies . . . Phillies.

The day it happened we all went to Mom's house so we'd be together. She made a big lunch, and we ate. Baked pork chops with apples, that potato salad he hated — no Oreos. We were handling it pretty well until the coffee came out. Then everyone lost control — crying, praise, self-pity. Except me. I couldn't manufacture tears. I don't know why. Everyone was hugging each other — like it was going to make up for something. Even that made me uncomfortable. They weren't hugging me, they were hugging my little brother. They were hugging Marc. . . . Senators.

You know what he liked? Baseball. I was never a real sports

34

fan — much less baseball — and every morning over cereal, little Marc would give me a dissertation on like how Lou Ghewig wasn't a natural, or why Babe Wuth was called "Babe." If it got to be too much, I'd just tune out. I tuned out a lot.

He would do the funniest things with his cereal. He'd pile it up on his spoon as high as it would go, and quick shove it all in his mouth like it was going to get away. No Cheerio could escape Marc. He got 'em all. (He starts to build a card house.) But he sure did like to talk in the morning. Either about baseball, or his army men, a steam shovel he saw, whatever. It's funny — those things really meant a lot to him. But how much could a twelve-year-old's army men mean to an almighty senior in high school? When I went off to college, I didn't give a whole lot to saying good-bye to Marc. I'm not too big on good-byes, anyway. I didn't think about what *I'd* be missing. I would miss the most important part of his life — liking girls, math problems. (He pulls one card from the foundation and the house gently falls.)

The night after the accident, I went for a walk and found myself at the duck pond. It was dark, and very quiet. I couldn't see the ducks. I listened. I listened. When I got home, I lost it. I ran from room to room crying and turning on the lights, hoping I'd find . . . I don't know . . . something. I never got to help him with his math. Not that he would never take geometry or trig, but that I would never get to help him with it. Yankees . . .

I wanted to open up and share with him before, but I always made it so complicated. I always ended up playing the condescending big brother with the "important lesson." Now I realize that *he* was trying to share — every morning while I was tuning out. But why couldn't I figure that out before? I'm supposed to be the smart one.

Little Marc. He wasn't going to be very tall. He was just hitting his growing spurt though. His small size sure didn't stop his big mouth. I can still hear him — Jackie Robinson. Yogi Bewa. It was a nice service, I guess. Sure was a small coffin.

I never listened. Did I get enough of a chance? Right. Is twelve years enough? Cubs . . . Cubs . . .

(He picks up the Cubs stack and gently sprays it across the floor.)

LIGHTS FADE

INTERMISSION — BILL ONE

TOMATOES I
By Ned Oldham

Bill One:	No. 9
Bill Two:	--
Bill Three:	No. 2
Lighting:	Full stage
Music:	Contemporary
Costume:	Apron
Props:	No special
Setting:	See script

Humorous
Male

(Piece begins offstage and entrance continues on the decant of the word "tomatoes." ACTOR goes C stage.)

ACTOR. Tomatoes, tomatoes, tomatoes, tomatoes, tomatoes . . . When will you ever learn? I've told you time and again to turn the disposal off when you are finished because it keeps the cat up, and you know about the cat. Silly tomatoes, silly, silly, silly, silly.

RED AIR
By Ruth Jacobson

Bill One:	No. 10
Bill Two:	--
Bill Three:	--
Lighting:	Full stage
Music:	19th Century Romantic Music
Costume:	In the style of Oscar Wilde
Props:	Tea cup
Setting:	Table and two chairs

Humorous
Male/Female

(LETITIA enters. She is dressed as for an Oscar Wilde tea party. She sits at the tea table and waits. CHARLES enters with silver tea tray, two cups, a silver pot, napkins, etc. He is wearing a smoking jacket and cravat tie. He sets out the tea and, raising a cup, speaks to LETITIA.)

CHARLES. Have some red air, my darling, my dear one.

LETITIA. Keep your red air to yourself. Go eat a cauliflower with your nose.

CHARLES. I have, I have.

LETITIA. And?

CHARLES. And?

LETITIA. The end result?

CHARLES. I had lice in my nostrils for a week. A very singularly messy business. You really should try some of this red air, my beloved.

LETITIA. I will not try your accursed red air, do you hear?

CHARLES. Peanuts are made for growing, and so are we.

LETITIA. Only peanuts?

CHARLES. Peanuts, us, and an occasional rodent.

LETITIA. Never could stand the beastly things.

CHARLES. Peanuts, rodents, or us?

LETITIA. Rodents, you pompous piece of furniture!

CHARLES. Ah, Letitia . . . you have wounded me to the quick! Letitia, Letitia . . . I'm drowning!

LETITIA. Are your lungs filling up with water?

CHARLES. Yes, yes!

LETITIA. Would you like some red air?

CHARLES. Yes, please!

LETITIA. Well, I shan't give it to you. No, I'm afraid you're much too beastly a boy to live, and so you must die . . . and you may thank me for it. (She stalks out as:)

LIGHTS OUT ON CHARLES

40

THE IN CROWD
By Michael Weiss

Bill One:	No. 11
Bill Two:	--
Bill Three:	--
Lighting:	Full stage
Music:	No special
Costume:	See script
Props:	See script
Setting:	See script

Humorous
Four Females/Three Males
One Male or Female

CAST

Four "ladies"	dressed in very fashionable cocktail clothes, each with a little purse
Three "gentlemen"	dressed in various fashionable outfits, one in a three-piece banker/doctor suit, one in a leisure suit, and one in turtleneck sportcoat — a rather aging preppy
One adolescent	dressed in *very* contemporary radical clothes such as: split jeans, boots, blue work shirt (wrinkled), etc.

(As the lights come up, the LADIES are grouped on one side of the stage, the GENTLEMEN on the other. All are slumped over at the waist, head to toe, like deflated mannequins. As the ADOLESCENT walks among them she touches each and they pop into frozen positions reflective of the gay, happy cocktail party circuit.

ADOLESCENT. They dress up in clothes that are the kind that need dry-cleaning. All the clothes they wear need dry-cleaning. They wear high-heel shoes — (LADIES snap one leg up.) — as fashion and to look taller than they really are. (LADIES snap legs down.) Little purses — (LADIES extend one arm on which hangs an evening bag.) — endowed with round gold sequins. (ADOLESCENT takes one purse and examines it.) The name of the designer is first and foremost. (ADOLESCENT replaces evening bag and the LADIES all snap arms back to pose.) The discussions consist of — husbands, wives, money . . .
GENTLEMAN NO. 3. Money!
ADOLESCENT. More money, clothes . . .
LADY NO. 1. Clothes!

ADOLESCENT. . . . sales . . .

LADY NO. 2. Sales!

ADOLESCENT. . . . shopping . . .

LADY NO. 3. Shopping!

ADOLESCENT. . . . other parties . . .

LADY NO. 4. Other parties!

ADOLESCENT. . . . dinner in fancy . . .

LADY NO. 4. Fancy!

ADOLESCENT. . . . restaurants and other shallow . . .

LADY NO. 3. Shallow!

ADOLESCENT. . . . conversations, all consisting of decadence . . .

GENTLEMEN NO. 1. Decadence!

ADOLESCENT. . . . and material . . .

LADY NO. 1. Material!

ADOLESCENT. . . . wealth. They don't like to go downtown, but if they have to go, they keep the doors locked, or make their husbands go with them. Inside the house, there are magazines out on the table where the guests can see them. The titles of the magazines are —

LADY NO. 2. *Bon Appetit*!

LADY NO. 1. *Vogue*!

LADY NO. 3. *Mademoiselle*!

LADY NO. 4. *House and Garden*!

GENTLEMAN NO. 2. *Time*!

GENTLEMAN NO. 3. *National Geographic*!

GENTLEMAN NO. 1. *Playboy*! (The LADIES whip around, shocked.)

ADOLESCENT. The *Playboy* is for the men . . . (LADIES resume poses. All the LADIES and GENTLEMEN in chorus repeat words with quick pose changes.)

LADY NO. 1. Value . . . material

LADY NO. 2. Crowded . . . surfaces

LADY NO. 3. Shallow . . . expensive

LADY NO. 4. Fancy . . . jealousy

GENTLEMAN NO. 1. Big . . . decadence

43

GENTLEMAN NO. 2. Consumption . . . excesses

GENTLEMAN NO. 3. Money . . . massive.

ADOLESCENT. They drive cars that are big . . .

GENTLEMAN NO. 1. Big!

ADOLESCENT. . . . and comfortable and expensive.

LADY NO. 3. Expensive!

ADOLESCENT. It doesn't matter that they require massive . . .

GENTLEMAN NO. 3. Massive!

ADOLESCENT. . . . amounts of gas to travel the shortest distances. Jewelry boxes contain excesses . . .

GENTLEMAN NO. 2. Excesses!

ADOLESCENT. Of gold jewelry, whose surfaces . . .

LADY NO. 2. Surfaces!

ADOLESCENT. . . . are crowded . . .

LADY NO. 2. Crowded!

ADOLESCENT. . . . with . . .

LADY NO. 1. Diamonds!

LADY NO. 3. Rubies!

LADY NO. 4. Emeralds!

ADOLESCENT. . . . and any other stone with considerable value.

LADY NO. 1. Value!

ADOLESCENT. It doesn't matter what this jewelry looks like — as long as it is expensive . . .

LADY NO. 3. Expensive!

ADOLESCENT. . . . and cause jealousy . . .

LADY NO. 4. Jealousy!

ADOLESCENT. . . . among friends. These are the people who attend at least seven cocktail parties a month, consuming . . .

GENTLEMAN NO. 2. Consumption!

ADOLESCENT. . . . a minimum of eight cocktails per party.

(LADIES and GENTLEMEN say their words. ADOLESCENT moves about touching each blabbing party person on the back. They drop suddenly into the pre-show slump. When everyone is still, the ADOLESCENT moves off and lights dim.)

DR. MONTY
By Ted Oldham

Bill One:	No. 12
Bill Two:	--
Bill Three:	--
Lighting:	No special
Music:	No special
Costume:	No special
Props:	No special
Setting:	No special

Humorous
Male

(The CHARACTER steps forward as the previous piece ends.)

CHARACTER. I just met Monty . . . Monty, the proctologist.
Nice old fellow. I don't know . . . I felt really bad from the
look on his face when I tried stalling from shaking his hand
. . . He was kind of funny, I guess, but . . . proctologist jokes
. . . "I once knew a woman with an asshole so big" . . . that
king of stuff. . . .

I really got the impression of dirty around him. He was nice-
looking, too, but it spoiled the whole effect when you found
out that he's a proctologist. He's married — bet he knows a
lot of hand-to-ass moves. I wonder what his wife thought . . .
"Hi, honey. How was work?" "Oh, fine, dear . . . had a
couple of people with some messy problems, but we got to
the bottom of them."

I wonder if he always wanted to be a proctologist. You
know, a life-long dream. I bet Monty had one of those little
baby-go-shits or whatever. But Monty's a nice guy, all right.

TOMATOES, TOMATOES – PART II
By Ned Oldham

Bill One:	No. 13
Bill Two:	--
Bill Three:	No. 2
Lighting:	Full stage
Music:	Contemporary
Costume:	Apron
Props:	No special
Setting:	See script

Humorous
Male

(The ACTOR enters and continues speaking to the audience as
  he clears away things on the set.)

ACTOR. When the cat is awake all he wants is Tender Vittles,
  and guess who feeds him . . . me. So that's right, buddy . . .
  yeah . . . keep the disposal off. Why do you use the disposal
  anyway? Liver, cereal, cabbage, beans, cantaloupe, escargot
  . . . fig newtons, you're stupid. You don't even need the
  disposal, yet you use it and keep the cat up.

THINKING PINK
By Ruth Jacobson

Bill One:	No. 14
Bill Two:	--
Bill Three:	--
Lighting:	Special No. 2
Music:	Contemporary
Costume:	See script
Props:	No special
Setting:	See script

Humorous
Female

(A GIRL, dressed in pink, walks hesitantly onto the stage that is bare except for one chair at C. She looks at the audience and giggles nervously as she waves slightly at them. She slowly crosses to the chair, stands beside it, and says nervously:)

GIRL. I'm here to talk to you about . . . about why . . . (She looks at the chair and asks the audience:) Is it all right . . . if I . . . sit . . . here? (As she trails off, she sits and looks around a little, still smiling. Then she begins:) I never could get things straight. I always missed the bus or was tardy to class. Mother always said I was the most disorganized person she ever met. She meets a lot of people, too.

So I guess it's only natural that I would flub up with my attempt. I read this article that said you're supposed to do it around X-mas, not in May. May is a beautiful, lovely month, with flowers growing and sun shining and lovers wooing. I guess it's only predictable that I'd screw things up. I mean, dropping the pills all over the floor was pretty silly. All those pills — I took 'em, but I'm not really sure why. I suppose I could figure out why, if I really *wanted* to . . .

Well, I guess I do. But it's not really a very good reason. I mean, I didn't try it because I was horribly depressed over some huge trauma, I mean, I just tried it because there wasn't anything better to do. I had this big pile of homework that I'd never finish in a million years, so, well . . . you know the rest . . . It always seemed so . . . romantic . . . to try suicide. When I think of Juliet killing herself over Romeo, I just get shivers. Of course, I could never stab myself. (Mimes stabbing herself in the chest.) That's very dramatic, but I'm sure it must not be the most pleasant sensation in the world. (She takes the "knife" out and drops it. She clutches at her throat.)

50

Hanging seemed kind of anticlimatic . . . (She drops her hands and points a finger like a gun.) . . . and guns are fine for men but women should use something a bit more genteel. That's why I decided on poison. The drama, the excitement of the unknown! Whether it will be quick or slow . . . it really adds this air of suspense to it all. (She mimes opening a medicine chest and taking out several bottles of pills.) I went up to my parents' medicine chest and set all the bottles of pills out on the vanity. I looked at all the kinds of pills . . . (She selects a "bottle.") . . . and finally I decided on these really pretty light pink pills in this oval shape with these light blue bands around them.

(She holds a "pill" up to her shirt.) They even matched what I was wearing! Well, anyway, as I already told you, I spilled almost half of them on the floor and I didn't use them because it's pretty disgusting to put something in your mouth that's been on the floor. Well, there were still a few left so I took 'em. Well, it turns out that you can't judge a book by its cover. Or you can't judge a pill by its color. I mean, they were pretty pills, but . . . well . . . they were water pills. Turns out that they didn't do anything that twelve glasses of water couldn't cure . . .

But that's it. That's my story. I wish I could help you more but I really can't think of a good, sad reason why I tried to kill myself. I . . . I hope you aren't *mad* or anything. I'd honestly tell you if there was any other reason. (She yells offstage to the Actor doing "Tomatoes.") I'm through now! (He answers from offstage.)

ACTOR (offstage). Oh, okay. I'll be there as soon as I get all these clothes in the washing machine. Talk to them a little longer.

GIRL. Well, thank you for your time. I'm only sorry I couldn't be of more assistance.

LIGHTS FADE

51

TOMATOES, TOMATOES – PART III
By Ned Oldham

Bill One: No. 15

Bill Two: --

Bill Three: No. 4

Lighting: Full stage

Music:

Costume:

Props:

Setting:

Humorous
Male

(The ACTOR enters.)

ACTOR. Come now, I'll tuck you in and read you a story and you'll go to bed because I have some work to do . . . Oh, wait, never mind, I have to clean off the air hockey table. Remember to pick up the sticks in the yard before you go to bed. And don't call me downstairs to undo your strap 'til seven o'clock. Remember, I work on Sundays, you don't. Have a good lunch, remember you are young yet and still tender. Oh, and by the way, Grandmother got a face lift.

QUICK LIGHTS OUT

BILL TWO

Pre-set: Choice of Director/Designer.

RED TENNIS SHOES
By Ruth Jacobson

Bill One:	--
Bill Two:	No. 1
Bill Three:	--
Lighting:	General
Music:	Contemporary
Costume:	Red high-top tennis shoes and baseball hat
Props:	No special
Setting:	No special

Humorous
Male/Female

From Back of House:

BOY. Stomp . . . stomp . . . stomp . . . stomp . . . stomp . . .

(A young BOY enters and stomps to C of playing space. He smiles at the audience, then looks down at his feet. He lifts his head and smiles broadly at the audience again.)

BOY. I look down at my feet and there they are. One, two. My two bright red tennis shoes. My tennis shoes are always down there, always on my feet, ready to run, run, run! I skip a little on the springy soles and my shoes skip with me, higher, faster, higher . . . skip, skip, skip.

Now my red shoes and I start to walk. We stomp in puddles and make them splash, stomp, stomp! We stomp on a big ant. Stomp! Stomp! The ant moves a little faster, so we stomp it again. Now we stomp at a big dog to scare it away. Go away, dog! Stomp! Now we hear Mommy calling, calling for us to eat lunch. Come on, shoes! Now we run, we run so hard and so fast that no one could catch us, so fast that we could outrun anyone, anyone at all . . . Then we go inside, my red shoes and me, and we slide into a seat at the table. Mommy says hello to us and serves us a peanut butter and jelly sandwich and milk. We eat our food and kick my sister under the table. Kick, kick, kick!

My sister starts to cry and Mommy tells us we're bad and makes us go to my room. Now we stomp very loudly – *stomp stomp stomp*! I slam the door and kick my red shoes off my feet – they got me in trouble. Then I cry very loudly so Mommy will hear . . .

(He cries loudly as LIGHTS DIM.)

FRIEND
By Will Crawford

Bill One:	No. 2
Bill Two:	--
Bill Three:	--
Lighting:	Area No. 1
Music:	No special
Costume:	No special
Props:	No special
Setting:	No special

Serious
Male/Female

(The ACTOR enters.)

ACTOR. When I was little, I climbed trees all the time, especially when something was troubling me or when I didn't get my way. They were things like – I couldn't watch T.V., or I couldn't have a Coke for dinner.

There was this big tree in our back yard . . . about a mile high, I used to think. At first it was real hard to climb. I would struggle up and get sap all over me. It was hard as hell to get off. Anyway, when I would finally get to the top, the branches at the tip-top would fork up and make a perfect seat for my little buns. What buns . . . I didn't have any. (He looks at his rear end.) I still don't. When I sat down in the seat, it was like I became part of the tree. I would sit up there for hours, just swaying in the wind. When I was up there I didn't think about the things that bothered me. Each time I climbed the tree it got easier. Soon the thrill was gone. I just got old, I guess.

I love little kids. Sometimes I wish I was a kid again. I think everybody does. That's why old people talk to themselves, because no one has time for them. Just like kids. All kids talk to themselves . . . because no one will listen. They act like they do, but they don't.

I got a call this afternoon. It was from the nursing home where my grandmother lived. She died. She was real sick. At least she won't suffer any more. She was the one person who listened to me when I was a kid. I guess because she was a kid, too. You know what I mean? She was the person who kept me during my parents' divorce. She always talked to me and took me to the park to let me climb trees when I was away from the big one at home. She knew.

Well, I'm going to go climb a tree. I'll see you.

58

ANIMAL SHELTER
By Traci Nall

Bill One:	--
Bill Two:	No. 3
Bill Three:	--
Lighting:	Area No. 2
Music:	Contemporary
Costume:	No special
Props:	School books
Setting:	No special

Serious
Female

(As lights come up we see a table C stage. A GIRL enters and we hear a school bell.)

GIRL. Mommie sends Little Monster, Jr. to his first day at the shelter. See how unwilling Junior is to go? He knows, he knows what this will be the beginning of. He knows that his days of confinement will never end. He knows that his psyche will be irreversibly warped. There will be no turning back now. No, Junior . . . no turning back now.

Once we are all in our cages, we are placed into groups. You over there, with them. I'll stay here. I don't want to be placed too close to another cage. I don't want to see how much I am becoming like you. I don't want to hear when we say the same things. I don't want to see when we start looking alike. So I'll just close my eyes and pretend. I'll pretend you're not here, that the cage is non-existent. I can pretend really well.

But, I can't pretend. I can see. I can really see that all this is just an animal shelter! That's all it is, just an animal shelter. Row upon row of bright shiny silver cages. Cages with bars where they put you. They leave you there. They feed you institutionalized material. They feed you structured material. Humph, what a diet!

I am to live on this material — "busy work!" My survival lies in the hands of my keepers. I either become one or die — become part of a "united body" my keepers say. Become part of a "united mind." One giant existing circle of thought and I must fall within the perimeter of this structure or perish as an outsider. I refuse. I am going to stay an individual. I don't want to become like you and everybody else. Forever locked in your cages.

Maybe I will die without the group. Maybe I can't survive.
60

But a future of roaming the empty halls of school, walking in and out of classrooms, blinded by the shine of the cages and sickened by the faces of the "pets" is a much better future than to live my total life emotionless in an animal shelter.

(Bell rings and the GIRL picks up books and starts to exit. She stops and goes back to the table. She throws her books on the table and exits in the opposite direction.)

DIRTY FINGERNAILS
By Laurie Kincade

Bill One:	--
Bill Two:	No. 4
Bill Three:	--
Lighting:	General
Music:	Sung by actress, zany contemporary
Costume:	See script
Props:	See script
Setting:	See script

Humorous
Female

(GIRL comes on wearing gloves and carrying beach items in a
    bag: two lawn chairs, a sun chin reflector, two magazines,
    etc. She is wearing a bikini bathing suit, large beach hat,
    sunglasses, and black leather gloves. She is looking for a place
    to sit and sun. She sings a careless melody and even whistles
    when she forgets the words. Follows mime of setting up her
    "nest," creaming her gloved hands, taking off her gloves,
    loosing her magazine, etc.)

GIRL. At age thirteen this started. I'm not sure how exactly.
    One day I just happened to glance down and there it was.
    There was dirt beneath my fingernails. I immediately searched
    around the room but no one else had dirt beneath their finger-
    nails. Even Luann Doyfstetter's fingernails had the black line
    of particles missing from them and everyone knows what
    she does when she's by herself. When I got home from school
    that day, I fled to the washroom and began scrubbing them
    and prying at them with a pair of tweezers but the filth ad-
    hered to my skin. I became so disgusted by the sight of them
    that I held my pencil in such a way that it gave me cramps
    after writing a while and made my writing illegible. At school
    I could always sense the eyes of my classmates focusing on
    me and my filthy fingernails.

One particular afternoon I came home so desperate that I
    seized a pair of scissors with the intention of cutting off my
    whole fingernail. Maybe then, I could really unearth that
    scum. But I didn't, because I was afraid it would hurt and
    that I would get blood everywhere and I didn't feel like
    being yelled at for being messy. Heaven knows, I'd had
    enough of that.

Looking back now, I realize how silly I was and I've gradually
    learned to accept my fingernails. My best friend, Louise, I
    discovered, always had worn gloves because she had thought
    that her hands looked older than everyone else's. Imagine,

I had never even noticed her gloves and even if I had, I probably would've thought her hands were cold or that she had had a wart frozen off, something like that. I'm glad I'm over that stage. Well . . . I do wear fingernail polish from time to time.

(Pause and then the GIRL slowly discovers dirt beneath her toenails.)

ONE OF THEM
By Traci Nall

Bill One:	--
Bill Two:	No. 5
Bill Three:	No. 1
Lighting:	Area No. 2
Music:	No special
Costume:	No special
Props:	Staged around cleaning up any leftover props and setting from previous monologue.
Setting:	No special

Tragicomedy
Two Actresses

(The TWO GIRLS enter.)

GIRL 1. Will they notice me?

GIRL 2. Isn't that what you want?

GIRL 1. Of course . . . not, silly. But it would be nice if they at least looked. Mother has always wanted . . .

GIRL 2. Mother wants what?

GIRL 1. What I want. What I . . .

GIRL 2. You want. Just like Mother.

GIRL 1. That's what everyone wants.

GIRL 2. Of course.

GIRL 1. Or needs.

GIRL 2. Of course.

GIRL 1. Which one are you?

GIRL 2. I am . . .

GIRL 1. One of those who wants to be noticed or one of those that needs to be?

GIRL 2. Just one of them.

GIRL 1. Oh, both? Isn't that somewhat . . . somewhat difficult at times?

GIRL 2. Not at all. It is quite easy to just be one of them. Simple, elementary. Just exist, not necessarily thinking, just exist and then you're one of them.

GIRL 1. But I thought that becoming . . .

GIRL 2. One of them.

GIRL 1. Involved many choices. Such as deciding which group to become.

GIRL 2. One of them.

GIRL 1. . . . How to act when you're . . .

GIRL 2. One of them.

GIRL 1. Or does the group you're in dictate your actions?

GIRL 2. And thoughts and clothing and . . .

GIRL 1. Everything else about you when you're . . .

GIRL 2. One of them.

GIRL 1. That's so. Mother always wanted me to . . .

GIRL 2. She always wanted you to . . .

66

GIRL 1. I am.
GIRL 2. What?
GIRL 1. One of them.

BLACKOUT

THE BOX
By Ned Oldham

Bill One:	--
Bill Two:	No. 6
Bill Three:	No. 6
Lighting:	Area No. 2
Music:	Contemporary Computer Sound
Costume:	No special
Props:	No special
Setting:	No special

Serious
Male

(The ACTOR enters in the darkness and begins speaking in the darkness.)

ACTOR. My dad has a box. It's little. About like this. (Quick lights up in small pool, revealing ACTOR sitting on a stool.) There's something in it, it's heavy, real heavy for being so small. I can't open it. It's locked and Dad's lost the key. He said that the thing that's in it doesn't have a name. He has the only one like it. The box stays in my dad's closet. It leaves little marks in the closet from the metal studs all over it. He'll never show me what's in it. I know he won't. He says he will, though. He says nothing important is in it. He won't show me, though. He says some day when he dies that I can have the box, but I don't want it. I just want to see what's inside, I think! Yes, that's all. I only want to see and I want him to show me. I don't want to have to see it by myself. I wonder why he won't show me? Nothing can be that good or bad, I don't think! It's not not being able to know what it is that makes me want to know. It's not my curiosity that makes it so bad. It's that my dad won't tell me. I wouldn't be satisfied if I found out what was in it. I need him to show me. It's his box. I'll get my own box and put something in it, then I'll lose the key.

QUICK LIGHTS OUT

LIGHT
By Traci Nall

Bill One:	--
Bill Two:	No. 7
Bill Three:	--
Lighting:	Area No. 1
Music:	Same contemporary computer sound as used for previous piece
Costume:	No special
Props:	No special
Setting:	No special

Serious
Female

(Small lighted space reveals a young GIRL lying on her side, facing the audience. She speaks the whole monologue from that position.)

GIRL. The light is starting to hurt my eyes. It reflects off of the things in the room, and it hurts my eyes. (She slowly closes her eyes, waits a moment, then abruptly opens them.) But the dark. I am afraid . . . I'm glad when it's day. The sunshine is so bright, so happy and comforting! I wish it would stay forever.

But the night frightens me. I know that there are things in the dark. Moving shapes and . . . and voices . . . and they frighten me. The dark is so cold and lonely. I don't like to be lonely. But during the day, I'm happy . . . happy and warm, and I am so lonely.

I saw my reflection in the glass last Tuesday after I woke up from sleeping. Someone played a horrible, nasty, nasty joke on me. Someone did it while I was asleep. Don't look at me! Someone played a terrible trick on me while I was asleep. They stole my mind and my eyes . . . my eyes that look just like my father's. He was a sea captain, but the waves, the waves took him away. The pranksters stole my mind and my eyes and put them in another body. A stranger's body!

I don't have my own hair, my own face, my own hands. They've all changed. All changed. So I don't look in the glass any more. No, I don't move the stranger's body except to light the candles when it gets dark. The candles. The candles are almost all gone. No light! They'll come back. But I won't move, not to push them away or call out. I'll be as still as the wax drippings that have fallen onto the floor from the candle. Cold and solid.

71

I don't sleep. I don't sleep because if I do the voices will get louder, the shapes will move faster and faster and then they'll take away my mind and my father's eyes and throw them, throw them far and hard.

So I don't sleep, but the light is starting to hurt my eyes.

LIGHTS SLOWLY DIM TO OUT

HAPPY BIRTHDAY
By Caroline White

Bill One: --

Bill Two: No. 8

Bill Three: No. 5

Lighting: Area No. 1

Music: Sung by actress

Costume: No special

Props: Scrapbook with appropriate props men-
                     tioned in script

Setting: No special

Humorous
Female

(Curtain pre-set open. Light comes up by way of a match lit in the darkness of a full-stage blackout. We see the face of a young GIRL in the light. She lights a birthday candle, and as the area spot slowly rises, we hear:)

GIRL (singing).
Happy birthday to Claire . . .
Happy birthday to Claire . . .
Happy birthday to Claire . . .
Happy birthday to me . . .

(Lights up full in spot. The GIRL holds one birthday candle in her hand, and she blows it out at the end of her song. Beside her are a litter of pictures, some birthday candles, and a scrapbook. The GIRL sits on the floor.)

GIRL. Sixteen . . . sixteen candles . . . I'm the only person my age in the world who's never been on a date. (She drops the candle and lights another, and begins to sing again.)
Happy birthday to me . . .
(Spoken.) Well . . . not a real date . . . (She blows out second candle.) I mean, like, I go to parties and movies with my friends, but no guy has ever called me up and asked me out . . . (She shuffles through her pictures. She finds a newspaper clipping of a high school athlete from the sports page. She practically faints at the sight of the picture as she begins gushing about him.) Oh, God, he's so gorgeous . . . (She shows the picture to the audience.)

His name's Ben, and he's got blond hair and bright blue eyes that make me melt every time I see him . . . (She gazes at the picture.) And one time I was standing in back of him in the lunch line . . . (She raises the picture slowly to her nose and inhales deeply.) . . . and I could smell his aftershave, even above the lasagna . . . it smelled . . . just like he should

74

smell. (She places the clipping in her scrapbook.) Anyway, Ben called me one Thursday night a few months ago . . . I was so excited! My stomach . . . my stomach did four flips. He asked me for the math homework . . . 'Cause he had slept through class . . . and . . . I knew it was just a way of starting the conversation. Well . . . it wasn't. He just said, "Thanks a lot. 'Bye." (She embraces a Pizza Hut menu from her scrapbook.)

Well . . . I have gone on a sort of date. It was set up . . . by my friend . . . my friend Jan . . . She got this guy she knows to come pick me up and take me to a movie and then to Pizza Hut. He was okay-looking . . . medium-tall . . . brown hair . . . brown eyes . . . Nothing special, but okay-looking. We didn't talk on the way to the movie or all through it . . . What can you say to someone you don't know? He didn't smell of anything, like . . . well . . . aftershave . . . No . . . a . . . bright blue eyes . . . When we got to Pizza Hut we had a deep dish pizza with pepperoni and mushrooms and sausage . . . and even anchovies . . . disgusting. But he wanted them . . . so we had them. And onions . . . on the first date . . . onions . . . God! We ordered, or rather *he* ordered . . . and then . . . well, silence. God! What to say! Well, *something* had to be said . . . so . . . I asked him what classes he was taking, and he said . . . (She takes a piece of paper from her collection and reads from it.)

". . . English, French, Pre-calculus, Physics . . ." (She flings the paper aside.) . . . or something incredible like that. And I said, "Oh." He didn't ask me anything. He just answered my questions . . . like he didn't even care about me. What a *dud*! I was bored to death! Why? Tell me why Jan would set me up with that *stud*! . . . er, I mean dud, dud . . . She must think I'm really desperate or something! I don't want her feeling sorry for me! It's not like I'm a social outcast or anything! (She hums a few bars of "Happy Birthday" while rummaging through her scrapbook.) I do go out with my friends, for God's sake . . . (She stops short.) But not with guys. I mean, on dates . . . I . . . a . . . guess . . . well, maybe . . . maybe they just don't like me . . . I'm not . . . desirable . . . I guess I'll just go through high school . . . without a . . . date . . . (She lights another birthday candle.) Maybe college, too . . . I just wait every day for *that* phone call . . . Everyone else gets them . . . (Lights slowly down.) Why not me? (She blows out the candle as:)

LIGHTS OUT

RUNAWAY
By Sandra Wucherer

Bill One: --

Bill Two: No. 9

Bill Three: No. 8

Lighting: Area No. 2

Music: Contemporary rock

Costume: Appropriate to character

Props: No special

Setting: No special

Serious
Female

(Lights up in small space on a young GIRL. She stands and simply speaks.)

GIRL. I ran away from home, I guess about two weeks ago. I can't even remember why any more. I guess just because I got in a fight with my parents. I hung out at this girl's house for a week. Her mother was out of town so we had fun throwing parties and getting wasted. Then I was lucky enough to meet this girl, Lana, who ran away, too. She was tough and it's so much better to stick with someone who's in the same shoes, and even better when they are tough. That way you don't have to be tough all by yourself.

That night I met her we decided we'd better leave town. The next day we hitchhiked to a town about a hundred miles away. Lana used to live there so she knew people we could stay with. We ripped off some shampoo from this store and washed our hair in a gas station bathroom 'cause by that time we were all grubby-looking. We met some of her friends and went over to somebody's house where they said we could stay.

The house was filthy. The dishes in the kitchen hadn't been washed for months. I never went in there again after one look. All the rooms had junk piled on the floor, at least a foot high. When I went to the bathroom there was no toilet paper and there were bugs. There were bugs everywhere in every room. There were about eight different people living there already. Most were guys, but they were nice, never tried nothing on me. I was glad 'cause they were older and ugly. One guy was about thirty — had hair that went all the way down his back, and he was big — must have weighed over three hundred pounds. I was scared of him but he was nice. One day I even braided his hair for him. We got drunk as shit almost every night there. I was glad when I got drunk. I remember the two nights we didn't get drunk. When everyone

78

fell asleep, I couldn't. Kept feeling bugs on me. I couldn't stop thinking of home, my cozy room where I was always so safe. I cried then, but no one knew. I just let the tears roll down my cheeks, but I didn't make a sound.

After a week at that house I called my mom, and when she answered the phone the tears came again. I asked her if she would pick me up and she said yes. She picked me up the next day. I told her to meet me in this bowling alley. So there I was waiting for her. I looked awful. Dirty and about twenty pounds skinnier.

Finally she came and we walked to the car, got in, and then those tears wouldn't stop. I said, "I'm sorry, Mom." And she said, "It's okay, baby. I love you and everything is going to be all right now." And I just kept crying, saying, "I love you," to Momma. It felt so good to be going home. And everything was all right, until the next fight when I ran away again.

LIGHTS DIM SLOWLY ON THE GIRL

SKIN FLICKS
By Michael Weiss

Bill One:	--
Bill Two:	No. 10
Bill Three:	--
Lighting:	Area No. 2
Music:	From previous monologue
Costume:	No special
Props:	Newspaper
Setting:	Bench

Serious
Two Male Actors

(When the play opens, BOB and JIM, two men in their twenties, are sitting, reading the movie ads in a newspaper.)

BOB. This one has got that girl, Candy, in it again.

JIM. I think after this one, I'll be tired of her.

BOB. I'm tired of her already. You'd think they'd get some new girls in these things instead of using the same old ragged-out ones.

JIM. Probably plenty of girls that would jump at the chance to be in one of these skin flicks. (He chuckles. Their focus is suddenly directed to the back wall of the theatre, indicating the beginning of action on the movie screen.) Shh, now be quiet . . . you know how I like to watch the previews. (They watch for awhile in silence.)

BOB. Why do you think Cathy called it off between me and her?

JIM. You know why . . . it's the same old reason. Now, no more — you know I don't like to talk about it.

BOB. It helps me.

JIM. Look, it's the same reason all the girls I started something with quit calling as soon as they found out what happened to me from the accident. That was it . . . we're having the same old conversation. Hell, you know what it's like. We both went through the nightmare together. It's not like coming to these damn things is something new. (There is a long pause with their attention directed to the screen.)

BOB. Goddamned job. There we were working our butts off, barely making enough to live on, and then . . . then the tank blew.

JIM (mad). Quit talking about it!

BOB. It helps me. (He imitates the explosion.) *Bam*! Blew up and left us both lying there half-burned up and nearly dead. I don't even remember riding in the ambulance to the hospital. I remember waking up, though, looking down at my legs and arms all burned up, hurting like I never hurt so bad in my whole life and looking over at the bed next to mine and seeing you in it looking just as bad as me. (He thinks for a

81

minute and begins to speak again.) Then Mr. Bossman comes in looking real sad and explains how a propane tank blew up right next to where we were working.

JIM. Would you just quit? *Quit!*

BOB (ignoring him). Yeah, looking real sad . . . that's all he was doing . . . just looking sad . . . he wasn't really. Hell, he was happy. Happy to be inside his office when it blew and not outside with us while we got burned . . . out there working our asses off and what did we get for it . . . *Burned up and scarred for life.*

JIM. Now you're gonna talk about how we lost our case and didn't get enough compensation. (Comforting him.) Don't you see, it's not helping you to talk about it. It just makes you feel bad to remember what we went through and don't you ever forget . . . we went through that *goddamned* explosion together. But now life goes on and we're gonna go through whatever else happens together, too.

BOB. Yeah, I guess you're right. But I can't help being mad about the whole thing. It wouldn't be right if I wasn't mad.

JIM. Hell, at least you know what it was like to love a girl, to have a chance to share your life with someone who cared about you . . . a girl who took you for who you were. Every time I get to the place with a girl where it's time to take my clothes off and make love, it's all over. She suddenly doesn't want me any more 'cause she can't stand to look at a body that's got scarred-up skin.

BOB. But, don't you see? That just makes it worse . . . to know what it feels like to have a girl love you and take you for who you are and all of that, because I know I'll never be able to have that again. Look at us. Do you blame Sue or Cathy or Diane for leaving? I don't know that I could love someone that looks so ugly . . . burn victims . . . freaks . . . that's what they call us.

JIM. I know that I could love any girl, as long as I was in love with what she was. Who cares what she looks like?

BOB (in a sarcastic, pissed-off tone). Well, let's sit back and get a cheap five-dollar thrill, since that's all we can get. (Again, their focus is drawn toward the movie screen. They watch for awhile before Jim speaks.)

JIM. I sure do like the way that Candy girl smiles.

LIGHTS FADE TO BLACK

ANGIE'S SONG
By Ruth Jacobson

Bill One:	--
Bill Two:	No. 11
Bill Three:	No. 7
Lighting:	Area No. 2
Music:	Brahm's "Lullaby" at end only
Costume:	No special
Props:	No special
Setting:	No special

Serious
Female

(Lights up on small space and young GIRL.)

GIRL. I guess I've always been of "dubious reputation" as my minister puts it. I never thought much about the rights or wrongs of it all when I was panting in the back seat of someone's car. It wasn't that I especially enjoyed it. If you want to know the truth, it was more like mild distaste. I never heard any bells. I don't know why I did it. I just didn't mind it. I got lots of friends that way, I guess.

I always was really careful — I was on the "pill" since eighth grade. I never missed it. But then — I don't know what happened. My dad started giving me a bunch of garbage about my life. He always does that, but it was really starting to bother me. It wasn't much — he'd slap me around a little and then tell me to go away — and I would. I'd go right to Steve's or Phil's or Mike's and just go to it.

Well, around that time I kind of stopped taking the "pill." I kept forgetting, and finally I ran out and didn't refill my prescription. I thought I could last a little while without it. Well, I sure didn't. When I found out I was pregnant I didn't cry. I don't know how I felt — kind of relieved. I didn't feel any of that "miracle of life" bull that you're supposed to. I just felt kind of relieved, like I'd finally done something right. I don't know. That's kinda dumb, I guess.

Well, my dad wanted me to get an abortion. I couldn't. I said I wouldn't and he got mad again. I racked him, and I mean *hard*, and I ran out of the house blubbering like a jerk. Later that night I called from a pay phone and Mom kept askin' me to come home. I had to. I didn't have a job or anything.

Everything went fine. Then I was getting really big, about six months along. My dad got mad. The toothpaste was missing. He got so mad he pushed me down the stairs — by accident. I screamed. It hurt so much — like someone taking a knife and scraping out your insides. I just kept screaming and screaming. I think I was bleeding. My mom called an ambulance, and I think I kept screaming until they clapped that mask over my face and whisked me away . . .

I had a fracture in my elbow. Angie wasn't so lucky.

She was so far along, they could see her face and everything. I didn't see it but I know she was very pretty. I know she was smart, too. When we were alone I would talk with her. She would bump around and I would talk to her and everything . . . she was a good kid, I know . . .

Now I just kinda walk around. Above it all. Nobody bothers me, nobody touches me. I still talk with my Angie. I don't know what I'll do. I don't know if I care. I don't know.

LIGHTS SLOWLY OUT

INTERMISSION

THE LAST GOODBYE
By Michelle Newman

Bill One:	--
Bill Two:	No. 12
Bill Three:	--
Lighting:	Area No. 2
Music:	Contemporary folk
Costume:	No special
Props:	Bottle of pills, vial of poison, glass of water, tape recorder and cassette
Setting:	Chair with small table

Serious
Male

(Lights come up on JAY, sitting in a chair. On the table next to him is a tape recorder, a glass of water, a prescription bottle of pills, a vial of poison, and a cassette for the tape player.)

JAY. Well, I guess this is it, folks. I know that this is a rather uncommon suicide note, but you've never been able to read my handwriting anyway. I know how rare an occasion it is that you ever listen to me and understand what I'm saying, but please try this time. I won't bother you again. You see, I've been very clever about this . . . you should actually admire the perfection of it. You especially, Mom, if you're not too drunk to understand it. And please, Dad . . . I know you want to put this out of your mind and go back to work, but try and listen to me. Force yourself. If you think that I'm doing this only to make you feel guilty, you're right. What other reason is there to leave a suicide message? Certainly not to explain my action. I don't have to justify myself to anyone.

Don't worry though. I'll give you all of my reasons. I like to keep an interested audience. You also know that I'm not leaving this out of concern for my belongings. If I were so worried about them, I'd have taken care of them before this. Thus we establish that I'm doing this to make you miserable. Don't turn me off yet or you'll miss the good part. That's when I get into the why's and wherefore's.

Now I'll go into the history of this dastardly act I have committed. I've thought about this since . . . oh . . . last year I would guess is the first time. I just had to think of the perfect way. I could always have bought a gun, but it seemed so messy. I thought of running out in front of a car, but what if it didn't work? My biggest problem was wrist slashing. You know how much I hate pain. They say it's painless if the knife is sharp, but just in case they were wrong I didn't want to risk it. I didn't want to die of agony before I bled to

88

death, if that makes any sense. Anyway, I resorted to what I did. Poison. It's quick, it's clean, but it's painful. Knowing how painful it is, I decided to take sleeping pills with it. Thus I'd be asleep through all the nausea and burning.

Aren't I brilliant? It's so simple. All I had to do was wait till you went away for a while. And you did, thank you very much! By the way, how was Greece? Never mind. Don't answer. I don't really care right now, anyway.

You know, what I did really deserves a round of applause. I think that what I did took more guts than anything you have ever in your life seen. Most people think that suicide is a horrible cowardly act. I just can't see it as that. When you're standing there with the pills in your hand, it'd be the easiest thing in the world to follow your instincts and flush them down the toilet! The hardest thing is to do the totally unnatural thing, the thing that you've been told that only lunatics do, the thing that scares the hell out of you . . . and take them.

Note, if you will, that I have been talking about myself in the past tense. I myself have just realized this. It is, of course, unintentional. If, however, you feel hurt by it, may I say now that I take full credit.

You're probably saying to yourself right now, "What did I do?" Well, now you get your answer. You are two parents that some people would absolutely adore having. You dote on me, you pamper me, and yet you don't spoil me. There is nothing on this earth that I've needed or wanted that I've had to do without. Kisses are one of the many things in abundance at our house. Yes, folks, it's all there — love, kisses, friendship, support, reliability, charm, sophistication, grace, worries, and hopes. They're all there. The only thing I think we've ever lacked is sincerity. Isn't it a pity that the one missing thing happens to strike me as the most important?

There's Mommy. So over-flowing with love, that it flows from her like water. Isn't it a shame that Mommy has to give her love to all the liquor store owners, too? Look at yourself, Mom. You're forty-three years old. In the mirror, though, you look like a fifty-year-old dying woman who thinks that drinking will make her young again. It certainly makes her feel young! That is, until the morning after, when she'll squeeze fresh orange juice for her first screwdriver of the day. Look, if you can't love yourself enough to care, do you expect me to believe that you love me?

Then, of course, there's Daddy. Or should I say, where's Daddy? You're as much of a workaholic as Mom is an alcoholic. Do you know why? I believe it's because you don't want to have to face us — your drunk wife and dead son. I know it's a pity that we never had time for that "man-to-man," but don't worry, sir. I didn't die a virgin.

Now you're saying, "Why didn't he come to us, and tell us?"

Why? Well, it's because you weren't the only reason for this. You were the top two, but not the only ones. A very good reason was failure. I've always felt like I can't do anything right. Another good reason is loneliness. You two saps always had each other, but who did I have? (He chokes back a sob.) I never forgave you for leaving me without any emotions other than hate. You know you did this when you made me live without honest love.

I hate you!

The final reason I've done this is because I got tired of waking up in the morning and seeing a pale, pitiful, helpless creature attempting to pull its life together every time I look in the mirror!

You may wonder how I can be so flip about this. It's because I'm glad that I've finally decided to take a definite action. This way at least I won't have to get up in the morning and ask, "Will I today, or not?" Well, this morning I said yes.

Well, this is it. I've no more to say. Look at me if you dare. You won't see regret on my face. Only contentment, and maybe nausea. If you wish to shut the tape off now, you can. Otherwise there's the "Unfinished Symphony" on the other side. Good-bye. (He places a note on the tape recorder which instructs his parents to play back the tape.)

LIGHTS GO DOWN AS
JAY LIFTS GLASS OF POISON TO HIS MOUTH

MY BROTHER
By Omar Shawkat

Bill One:	--
Bill Two:	No. 13
Bill Three:	--
Lighting:	Area No. 1
Music:	Contemporary
Costume:	No special
Props:	No special
Setting:	No special

Serious
Male and Female

(Lights come up on a MAN and WOMAN seated on stage. [The woman does not need to speak.])

MAN. My brother and I were real close. I've never known any other brothers that were best friends besides us. I really loved him — he admired me and I admired him. Both of us were model kids — we did well in school, were polite, never got out of line or caused any real problems. And we were real athletic, fierce competitors! Our specialty in sports was track. Phil was the state's best cross-countrier and I was top sprinter and hurdler. Phil was obsessed with running — he ran ten miles a day — religiously. He was an addict. To him, everything related to running. Running was an analogy for life to him . . . keep running, get better, get stronger, build stamina. Stamina . . . that was the key to his insanity. Nobody saw what was happening, not even me. All the people around him . . . his brother, his family, his friends, everyone who claimed to love him, never really were close enough to realize. Phil was always philosophizing about how everyone needs to develop their physical and mental stamina. Well, Phil had all the stamina in the world as far as running was concerned, but he wanted more . . . he wanted pain stamina . . . he wanted to raise his pain threshold. It started out with little things, like not caring about cuts, or sprains, or anything. Just an outright loss of respect for his own body. He started refusing medication of any kind — aspirin, cough medicine, antihistamines, or anything which is considered the easy way out. Now, it is so obvious — what he was doing. From here he went to other things to increase his "stamina." One time I remember Phil went to the dentist to get a couple of cavities filled. He immediately saw this as a chance to test himself, and he told the doctor not to use any novacaine. I remember him beaming with self-satisfaction afterward. His stamina was definitely strengthening. Soon, bruises and broken bones from his little accidents became more frequent. He even joined the football team, the perfect place to encounter pain.

Not long after joining the football team, Phil began applying his philosophy to his own mind, trying to better his own ability to accept and deal with mental stress and pressure. At night, just before going to sleep, he'd ask me things like, "What if Mom and Dad were killed?" or "What if I suddenly became paralyzed and couldn't move anything?" His imagination was always conjuring up wild situations and then he'd place himself into the situation. I guess he just started letting it get to his head. Almost every night he'd wake up screaming, or in a cold sweat after some nightmare.

But I never thought ol' Phil had any real problems. He was such a great guy. One day, all of a sudden, Mom comes into my room, says she just took Phil to the doctor — a psychiatrist. Calmly, she tells me that Phil is "neurologically manic-depressive" and is going to need "professional" help for a long time to come.

It was so blatantly obvious. And it happened right before my eyes.

NOT NORMAL
By Wolf Knapp

Bill One: --

Bill Two: No. 14

Bill Three: --

Lighting: Area No. 2

Music: Contemporary punk rock

Costume: Appropriate to character

Props: No special

Setting: No special

Serious
Male

(At the opening, the ACTOR is crouched at C against the back wall of playing space in small light. He plays the monologue in that light, rising and dropping his body as the action demands.)

ACTOR. On the bus you feel like exploding. All you can do is sit there and watch the mediocre people. They don't even seem to think enough to be phony. And you're such a chicken-shit you don't do anything about it. Just sit and stare and get nervous when they stare at your funny clothes . . . even though you know you are better than they are.

You get home, drink something, fall asleep in front of the telly, then fall asleep between the speakers, and when all else fails, fall asleep in Chapter One of *The Greek Way*.

You're not really tired. It's just that there's nothing to do. You can eat dinner and be civil to the family because they don't mind your weirdness. You can sit and wonder why you can't do anything. Then you go to a movie with some friends. You go with them 'cause they understand why you think the way you do, but they don't really think that way. You wish there were others around who think the way you do.

You always go to a movie because there is nothing better to do. Even a bad movie is better than sitting around at home. After the movie you go to someone's house and talk and drink. Drinking's okay. It's just that it lessens the explosion feeling. You can make the explosion feeling stronger if you do speed. That's good at parties where people are more likely to get on your nerves. You can feel your whole body tighten up and your brain goes into high gear and it's easy to hate things and people and yourself. Then you know that some day you really will explode.

After the movie or party you come home and watch T.V. and drink some more. Then you go to bed and wish you had exploded. You know that when you just think about it, it doesn't prove anything. If you really would stand up and yell at the people on the bus, or throw a chair through the window at school, you would be doing something . . . you might wake somebody. You would know you were a person.

Then you wake up with a headache and you see things through a mild haze. The haze disappears on the bus when you begin to hate all the apathetics riding with you. Then you get bored for a few hours. Then, if you are lucky, you go to a store or movie or someone's house and sit around. You take the bus home and you still haven't exploded.

You get on the bus feeling normal. You ride for a while just watching the people. You don't have any real reaction. Then a tremendous feeling of oldness fills you. You think the spirit is gone. You don't even care any more. Just like the old people. But it's not that way . . . it can't be. You're only seventeen. You have lots of time.

You start to really look at the people. They're just sitting and staring or reading or wondering if they will do good at work today. You're not going to be like that. They don't have any reactions. They don't see anything. They don't look for anything. They just exist. They don't have enough control to be alive. You won't be that way. They can't make you. You look up again. They are sitting the same way. But they won't be for long. They will have something special today. Say something! THINK SOMETHING! One old lady looks up. "Do you fuckin' exist? Do you ever think of how bored you are? Are *all* of you senile? DO SOMETHING!" Your backpack flies toward the window across the aisle. It crashes against the window and falls down between the businessmen. One of them tries to pick it up for you. You grab it. "Don't you feel it now?" The bus is stopping. You rip your backpack open. Books sail in all directions.

"YOU'RE THE FUCKIN' LOONEYS. I'M DOING SOME-THING! YOU'RE JUST SITTING THERE! FUCKIN' APATHETIC JERKOFFS! YOU JUST SIT THERE ROTTING AWAY! YOU'RE FUCKIN' TERRIBLE!"

The bus driver, a shortish, pudgy man, is walking back toward you. Most of the people on the bus are just staring as they usually do. Even the ones that got hit on the head with a textbook just turn and look before returning to their ignorant bliss. The bus driver is trying to pull you toward the front of the bus. You hit him on the head with *Man and Religion: Four World Views*. He lets go and stares.

"I'm getting off soon. I HOPE I'VE MADE YOUR DAY A LITTLE MORE INTERESTING! GO FUCK YOURSELF! GO TO WORK, GO HOME, GET DRUNK! YOU'RE A BUNCH OF FUCKIN' ZOMBIES! THINK! GODDAMNIT! REACT! I'M SCREAMING AT THE TOP OF MY LUNGS AND YOU JUST SIT THERE! GORMLESS! THAT'S WHAT YOU ARE! G'BYE AND FUCK OFF!"

You've been walking around downtown Louisville for an hour and a half. Nothing's really changed. You haven't come to any decisions about life. You're still bored and you still don't want to do anything. It still looks hopeless. You get to class. You listen to an old person lecture on the pros and cons of the fifth line of the twenty-third page of a twenty-five-hundred year-old play. You did something today. What? Provided some mild interruption for a bunch of hopeless old bastards. It was about as important as this fuckin' play. You're getting angry again. You know it's useless. (He laughs.) BUNCH OF FUCKIN' ZOMBIES! APATHETIC JERKOFFS! ROTTING AWAY!

It's all fuckin' hopeless. That's the funniest part.

You take a bus home. You drink something. You watch T.V. You don't know if you can take it much longer. Something better happen.

Hopeless . . . hopeless.

LIGHTS OUT

UNPRODUCED

NEW MATERIAL

RECESS
By Traci Nall

(Lights up in small space, revealing a teacher's desk and chair. An ACTRESS stands beside it. A school bell rings. She improvs instructions to her class to ready them for recess, careful to ask the last child to close the door after them. She stands motionless a moment, then slowly opens a drawer in her desk and pulls out a doll.)

ACTRESS. Do you know what I see in your cheeks, m'dear? I can see them plain as day . . . they're right there in your chubby, cutesy-cutesy cheeks. No, don't be afraid. I won't hurt you. There, that's better. I once had a little girl, too, you know. A little girl all of my own. I dressed her, fed her, took her for walks. Why, we did everything together. Would you like to do that? Huh? Would you? I'm all by myself and I really want to take care of you. Oh, sure. I see them. I see them walking through the halls, playing out on the playground. I hear their light, laughing voices. And, sometimes their laughter becomes so loud, so loud that I just want to scream to make it stop. Stop! Stop! Please, oh, please stop! You're hurting my ears! Oh, please stop!

The pain hurts so much. So much that I have to close my eyes and wish it away. Go away and leave me alone. See, my eyes are closed. But when I open them again, I see your pretty, chubby little cheeks. And I just have to smile because the pain's all gone and I know, I know that you'll stay here and protect me from the pain. You will, won't you? Yes, stay and keep the pain away. That's it, smile for me. Smile so I can see your chubby, cutesy-cutesy cheeks!

(The bell rings. She quickly puts the doll away in her desk. She stands smiling as the lights dim.)

THERE'S NO WINNER IN A TIE GAME
By Omar Shawkat

FEMALE 1. Oh, Mother . . . they got us, they got us.

FEMALE 2. A heartless lot they are.

FEMALE 1. Worse than heartless . . . they're, they're . . . unfeeling.

MALE 1. Mm-mm-mmmm . . . Those women sure were sightly dishes . . . Smooth, shapely, sensuous creatures. Long strands, bouncing freely, draping leisurely over her shoulders and flowing onward down her splendid spine. It's almost a pity that . . .

MALE 2. No, we've done our job well.

MALE 1. Yes, that's true . . . I guess . . . yes, indeed we have.

FEMALE 2. You must remember, my dear, you must always remember, for comfort's sake, that we still — shall I say — have them in our noose.

FEMALE 1. Mom, Mom, Mom — must you talk in riddles?

FEMALE 2. Forgive me, dear. My mother told me when I was about your age — so it is time I told you.

FEMALE 1. What is it?

FEMALE 2. What is what?

FEMALE 1. Oh, Mother, you can be facetious.

FEMALE 2. I am sorry. Please accept my apologies.

MALE 2. Still, though, you have a point. Females were such beautiful creatures.

MALE 1. Yes, indeed — beautiful, beautiful.

FEMALE 2. You see, my dear, males are quite, quite jealous creatures.

MALE 2. But we must admit, it was well worth it. They were getting way out of hand.

FEMALE 2. Our primitive types — in decades past — did at one time enjoy arousing this and other senselessly typical male emotions — a sort of game, I suppose. And, through the years, we have come to recognize that males are quite inferior, as their susceptability to become emotional shows.

MALE 1. We planted the seed early, that's why we're superior.

MALE 2. One of the many reasons.

FEMALE 2. We stopped enjoying tantalizing men and started to — actually started thinking of them — as quite stupid.

MALE 1. That's what it takes, planting the seed for the destruction, the crushing of an uprising. Anticipation is the key. We could feel it coming. We never knew why — what triggered the feeling. But, in the long run, we have triumphed.

FEMALE 1. That is intriguing.

FEMALE 2. As the two races drifted apart and we asserted our superiority, we again, however unwittingly, aroused the male jealousy.

FEMALE 1. I do hate males. Test tubes are so handy.

FEMALE 2. Anyway, men obviously have long been aware of our rise and that we could prove "dangerous." They had the intelligence, however meek, to attack our one weakness — our feet.

MALE 2. Posterity will condemn us.

MALE 1. Nonsense.

MALE 2. They just won't understand our position.

MALE 1. Mm-mmm.

MALE 2. Lovely things they were . . . females. It's a pity they're so feminine.

MALE 1. Indeed.

MALE 2. Look! Don't their feet look so innocent, so . . .

MALE 1. But deadly!

FEMALE 1. Sometimes I wish I had hooves.

FEMALE 2. But you are young, your mind will alter.

MALE 2. Who would have imagined that a pair of patent leather, ruby, uncomfortable, unfitting Florsheim's could alter — could so completely change an entire species.

FEMALE 1. But do go on.

FEMALE 2. Yes. They used the dreaded high-heels to ruin us.

MALE 1. A new breed. Genetic alteration.

MALE 2. A mutation.

MALE 1. Phenomenal. And so, we have the last laugh.

FEMALE 2. So they thought. Now I will share with you what my mother told me. Although we have lost the battle, we haven't lost the war. We have a weapon — a deep-rooted defense mechanism.

FEMALE 1. What do you mean?

FEMALE 2. Planted centuries ago —

FEMALE 1. Tell me, tell me, tell me!

FEMALE 2. The necktie . . . those snugly fitting snares which have, generation after generation, hung from the necks of males. The noose. Forever compressing their gullets, pulling down, down, down.

FEMALE 1. Do you mean . . . ?

FEMALE 2. Yes . . . stooping lower and lower. And their heads constantly compressing the narrowing circumference of their necks.

MALE 2. Foolish, foolish women. We even warned them. We said that flat soles would be much better.

MALE 1. They wanted it themselves.

MALE 2. They must have.

FEMALE 1. And reduced to neckless stoops.

FEMALE 2. Within fifty years they will be back on our level.

FEMALE 1. Themselves mutations!

FEMALE 2. Success is inevitable.

FEMALE 1. Marvelous.

MALE 1. Started their own nation. Population started declining at unheard of rates.

MALE 2. Phenomenal.

MALE 1. We put them in their place.

MALE 2. Justly so.

MALE 1. Let's proceed to the ward.

MALE 2. They are so tame.

FEMALE 2. Well, dear, you'll have to contemplate these new thoughts on the rack. I think I'll spend a full hour on it today. I'd really like to have my pelvic bones horizontal before I

die.
FEMALE 1. Like in the old days?
FEMALE 2. Yes, honey . . . like in the old days.

END OF "GLIMPSES"

DIRECTOR'S NOTES

DIRECTOR'S NOTES

DIRECTOR'S NOTES

DIRECTOR'S NOTES

DIRECTOR'S NOTES

DIRECTOR'S NOTES

DIRECTOR'S NOTES